Jacobean and Early Bourbon Fashions

TOM TIERNEY

DOVER PUBLICATIONS, INC.
Mineola, New York

Introduction

The term "Jacobean" is derived from "Jacobus," the Latinized name of James I, King of England. It is often used to describe the era of James's reign (1603–1625), in which the preceding Elizabethan mode was phased out in favor of a return to classical Renaissance style in many branches of design, including fine art, architecture, literature, and fashion. The leader of this transitional movement was Inigo Jones, an architect and painter commissioned by James's wife, Queen Anne of Denmark, to design a series of extravagant masques and plays for the entertainment of the court. It is primarily due to Anne that the Jacobean style was brought in as the next step beyond the lavish Elizabethan look. The heavy ornamentation and exaggerated silhouettes were gradually scaled back to a more understated look, which focused on the richness of fabrics. However, elements of Elizabethan clothing (which, in turn, borrowed heavily from Spanish fashion of the time) were still quite visible until the latter years of James's reign.

James's son, Charles I, took the throne in 1625 and married Henrietta Maria, the sister of France's king, Louis XIII, shortly thereafter. Charles was a patron of many notable artists, including Flemish painters Anthony Van Dyck and Peter Paul Rubens, both of whom he brought to England as court painters. The influence of Flemish and French fashions can be seen in his portraits by Van Dyck. His reign was tumultuous at best, thanks to never-ending quarrels with Parliament and the Puritans, poor advice from his advisors, and a civil war. He was tried by a high court, convicted of treason, and beheaded in 1649.

Across the channel, Henry IV ruled as the first king of France in the Bourbon dynasty, which would last for two hundred years. Ascending the throne in 1589 and reigning for twenty-one years, he devoted his patronage to the vitalization of Paris, commissioning the creation of the Tuileries gardens, the long gallery in the Louvre, and Place Dauphine. During most of his reign, the court fashions were primarily influenced by the Spanish styles as interpreted by his wife, Marie de Médicis, as well as those from Flanders and her native Italy. After Henry IV's assassination in 1610, nine-year-old Louis XIII became king with his mother acting as regent until 1617. He later depended on the Cardinal de Richelieu to advance his belief that his power as king was a divine and absolute right. During his reign, which lasted until 1643, fashion in France was marked by the popularity of lace and simple lines. Leather boots and ribbon-tied knee breeches (replacing puffed trunk hose) became standard for men, as did long hair topped with decorated hats—the "cavalier" look. Women's dresses dropped their necklines and cinched bodices even tighter, with hoopskirts remaining moderate. The prince and future king of France, Louis XIV, would later have an illustrious reign that ushered in the grand Baroque style of the late seventeenth century.

NOTE: Descriptions of unfamiliar fashion terms can be found on page 46.

Bibliographical Note

Jacobean and Early Bourbon Fashions is a new work, first published by Dover Publications, Inc., in 2004.

DOVER *Pictorial Archive* SERIES

International Standard Book Number: 0-486-43333-1

Manufactured in the United States of America
Dover Publications, Inc., 31 East 2nd Street, Mineola, N.Y. 11501

King James I of England, ca. 1610

The monarch for whom the Jacobean period was named wears a doublet with falling band collar, a jeweled cape, and paned, jewel-studded trunk hose over knee-length canions with ribbon garters. Hose and slip-on shoes with decorative shoe roses complete the outfit.

Anne of Denmark, Queen of England, ca. 1610

James's queen is wearing a richly patterned silk gown decorated with a high standing collar and intricate lace cuffs. The dress is worn over a French wheel farthingale (which took its name from its cylindrical shape) reinforced with spokes.

Man and Women of the Mercantile Class, ca. 1600

These Londoners are wearing small ruffs to accessorize their modest clothing. The women's gowns have short, puffed sleeves and lack the farthingale and bum roll foundations found in upper class fashions. The man's coat features long, hanging sleeves trimmed in fur.

Young English Nobles, ca. 1605

These brothers wear black taffeta doublets, trunk hose, and canions over knit hose. The whisk collar and cuffs are trimmed with point lace. Their outfits are topped with beaver hats.

Jamestown Settlers with a Native American, ca. 1607

Named after the king of England, Jamestown was the first British settlement in the New World, occupied mainly by the military. **Left:** Native American in loincloth and beads. **Center:** This musket man wears chain mail, wide breeches, and high, cuffed boots. **Right:** This commanding officer is dressed in a jerkin and trunk hose, with a ruff at his neck and knees. Among the relics excavated at Jamestown was a pleating iron for ruffs.

English Royal Children, ca. 1610

Left: Dressed in the style of her elders, the princess wears a striped silk gown with a wheel farthingale and a standing lace whisk. **Right:** The prince wears a braid-trimmed gown with a falling ruff. He holds early versions of a golf club and golf ball.

King Henry IV of France, ca. 1610

The French king wears a small ruff, doublet, and Spanish slops over knitted hose and shoes with lace shoe roses.

Dutch slops (also called German plunderhosen) are similar, but fall below the knee.

France's King Henry IV and Queen Marie de Médicis in Formal Court Dress, ca. 1610

Left: Henry wears a buttoned, fitted doublet with a short peplum and epaulets at the arm scythe. His paned trunk hose are of the same brocaded satin as the doublet. He wears silk stockings, shoes with large ribbon shoe roses, and a hat with a wire-frame crown. **Right:** The queen wears a corseted doublet with expanded wings and a gathered peplum over her farthingale-styled skirt. Her sleeves are padded and end in lace-edged cuffs. A padded satin crown finishes her outfit.

France's Queen Regent Marie de Médicis and King Louis XIII, ca. 1611

Left: The queen wears a satin gown ornamented with galloon (heavy gold braid) and pearls. Her *collet monte,* or wired standing collar, is made of cambric and point lace. In her hair, she wears a coronet of drop pearls.

Right: The youthful king is dressed in a doublet with a padded roll peplum and epaulets, padded sleeves with slashings, and striped satin Spanish slops over canions and silk stockings.

English Gentlemen, ca. 1614–16

Left: This elegantly dressed man from 1614 wears a flow-ered silk doublet with a lace whisk collar and a scalloped gorget. His brocade Spanish slops are fastened with points tied in bow knots pulled through the peplum at the waist. One of his boots is turned down to expose his knit stocking. **Right:** This gentleman, dressed in the style of 1616, models a doublet edged with gimp, with sleeves to match. His slops are embroidered with a celestial pat-tern, and are worn over silk stockings and shoes with lace shoe roses.

French Lady of the Court, ca. 1615

This ensemble includes a corseted bodice with lace inserts, a gathered lace peplum, and epaulets. The sleeves are slashed to expose undersleeves with lace inserts. The full skirt is stiffened with rows of stitching around the hemline and down the front. Her standing collar is wired and trimmed with lace. Her upswept hairstyle leaves tiny ringlets to frame her face.

King Charles I of England, ca. 1615

Based on a painting of the then-Prince of Wales, this costume features a lightly padded doublet with matching sleeves. The peplum of the doublet is cut longer, giving the illusion of a lengthier torso. His full Spanish slops are worn over silk hose and are fastened with satin ribbon garters. His whisk is made of cambric and lace. The mode of this period was heavily influenced by French fashion, likely due to the alliances of the French and English ruling class.

12

England's Queen Anne in Hunting Attire, ca. 1617

The queen wears her corseted bodice cut low in the new "exposed" fashion, accented with a lace-and-lawn-wired whisk. Her tall beaver hat is festooned with ostrich plumes. Short, open sleeves are sewn onto the tabbed epaulets of her gown, exposing her full, slashed undersleeves.

Queen Regent of France, Marie de Médicis, ca. 1617

Marie de Médicis wears an immense petalled ruff of stiffened white cambric over a black taffeta mourning dress. Over her gown, she wears a sheer black conque with wired wings.

French Couple in Court Dress, ca. 1617

Left: The lady wears a bodice with deep décolletage with a sheer fill, in the "exposed" fashion of the period. From beneath her epaulets fall hanging sleeves which open to reveal her slashed undersleeves and cuffs. The farthingale is now becoming passé, only worn by older women on highly formal occasions. **Right:** The gentleman wears a doublet with vestigial hanging sleeves and a falling ruff. The peplum of his doublet is cut into skirt tabs, which make it easier to get to the ties that fasten his slops. His tall leather boots are edged at the tops with scallops.

English and Dutch Gentleman at Court, ca. 1620

Left: The Englishman wears an ensemble of doublet and slops of brocaded satin that match the collar and lining of his velvet cape. His full slops are known as Venetians.

Right: The Dutch gentlemen is similarly garbed, with the exception of wearing a wired whisk in lieu of a pleated ruff. He wears a broad-brimmed beaver hat with plumes.

French Court Clothes, ca. 1620

Left: The lady wears a ribbon-trimmed taffeta bodice and sleeves, and a solid taffeta overskirt pinned up to reveal a brocaded underskirt. She carries a matching fabric muff with fur trim. Her collar is of lingerie fabric, sewn with tucks for shape and stiffening. **Right:** The gentleman wears a slashed, buttoned doublet with epaulets. His sleeves are paned, as are his slops. He wears Russian leather scallop-topped boots over his canions.

French Lady of the Upper Class in a Walking Dress, ca. 1620

This wealthy lady is wearing a promenade gown featuring a tucked and embroidered scalloped lingerie collar with matching double cuffs. Her underskirt is of embroidered lingerie fabric, as are her paned undersleeves. The overskirt and oversleeves are of brocaded satin. The bodice, gown, and sleeves are lavishly trimmed with ribbon and pearls. She wears a mask to protect her face from the sun.

English Upper-middle-class Family, ca. 1620

This young family is dressed in its finest. The father wears a *gullila,* or Spanish-styled starched collar, and a shirt with a lace-trimmed bib front. The outfit is completed with a short-sleeved jacket and Venetians. The mother's bodice has attached short sleeves over longer lingerie sleeves with triple lace cuffs. She wears a falling ruff at the neck. The seated child wears a scalloped triple ruff and the other wears a lace whisk. In this period, small boys and girls were dressed alike in loose gowns.

King Louis XIII of France and Charles de Luynes, ca. 1620

Here we see the king (left) and his companion enjoying pinches of snuff, a new import from the American colonies. By this time, the "cavalier" look had developed in France, which was the world's fashion leader. The corseted shape was discarded in favor of a waistcoat with sleeves and the ruff had been replaced by a falling band edged with lace, often referred to as the Louis XIII collar. The waistcoat's sleeves were generally slashed, expos-

ing the shirt. The shirt gained visibility because the waistcoat was often left open in the back, and the lower buttons left unfastened in front. The king's cloak is trimmed with gold galloon. It was considered impolite not to wear a cloak at this time. The bows and loops at the bottom of the breeches were now called cannons. Shorter, wide-topped, bucket-shaped boots became the vogue.

French Middle-class Couple, ca. 1624

Left: The man wears a tabbed doublet over slops, and canions with ribbon garters and hose. His cloak features the new Brandenberg style of fastening, using braid and buttons. **Right:** The woman wears a leather bodice over a short-sleeved jacket, to which she has buttoned on longer sleeves. Her blouse, of lingerie fabric, has a wide tucked and stiffened collar matched by the sleeve cuffs. Her apron is tucked into the bodice.

English Noble Couple, ca. 1624

Left: The lady wears an ornate lace bodice with matching sleeves and underskirt. Her overskirt is of velvet edged with lace, as are the long trailing sleeves and train. She wears a small ruff high on the neck, under which is a yoke made of lace, ribbon, and lawn. Hanging from her waist is a fan, an important accessory for a lady. **Right:** The gentleman wears an outfit of dark taffeta with gimp trim. His ruff and cuffs are edged with lace, and his doublet has tabbed wings and peplum. The full Spanish slops are held up by a row of ribbons laced through the peplum, and are worn over wrinkled canions tied off with wide ribbon garters over silk hose. His shoes are satin with taffeta bow ties.

French or English Middle-class Men, ca. 1624

Because most middle-class folk wore used clothing that had been discarded by the nobility, there were many interesting combinations of styles. **Left:** This man wears a fluted falling band and a capelike cloak with hanging open sleeves, a variation of the mandillion (or tabard).

This was a garment that would become popular with the Puritans. **Right:** This view of a middle-class man shows a doublet with wings at the shoulders and vestigial hanging sleeves, paired with an older-style wheel ruff. Both men wear slops.

French Court Couple in Promenade Dance, ca. 1625

Left: The lady wears a tightly corseted bodice with tabs, topped with a broad, tucked and starched eyelet-lawn collar. Her sleeves are slashed to reveal satin undersleeves and her overskirt is open in front, coatlike, to reveal a satin underskirt. On her head she wears a fine linen head-cloth. **Right:** The cavalier wears his broad-brimmed beaver hat with plumes, a love lock, and a lace-edged Louis XIII falling collar. His jerkin has slashed sleeves and tucked lace-edged cuffs. The band of bows at his waist are ribbon points, pulled through eyelets and tied to support his breeches. His jacket and breeches are decorated with gathered ribbon and beads. Ribbon garters and lace shoe roses finish his festive costume.

Rear View of a "Nouveau Riche" Middle-class Cavalier and Lady

Left: This illustration shows that the back of the man's jerkin is left unfastened to reveal his shirt underneath. He has ribbon cannons below the knee and wears lace boot hose. His tabard is worn like a cloak. **Right:** The lady wears the popular high-waisted corset, decorated with bands of gimp. Her voluminous three-quarter-length oversleeves are padded, with the undersleeves and cuffs showing below. The overskirt has narrowed from earlier styles, now worn as two panels hanging at the sides to reveal much of the petticoat, front and back. She wears a broad, stiffened lingerie collar over a pleated fall. A knitted roll or band is worn atop her braided hair.

French "Nouveau Riche" Middle Class, ca. 1625

The two ladies wear tightly corseted bodices with voluminous attached sleeves and horizontal stand-up collars, exposing much of the shoulder and collarbone. It became fashionable to pin up the overskirt on both sides, revealing richly made petticoats. The gentleman wears a paned doublet with a satin baldric across his chest and a silk sash around his waist. The tabbed peplum of the bodice has lengthened to almost the length of a modern suit coat. His plunderhosen, which fall below the knee, are padded for fullness, and he wears bucket-topped boots with large spur leathers. He wears a fluted falling band and has arranged a love-lock of his hair to drape on it.

Rear view of French Cavalier, ca. 1629

The cavalier's jacket is opened down the back—as are the sides of his breeches—probably to give more ease and freedom when mounting and riding a horse. The points at the top of his breeches are attached under the tabs of the jacket skirt and left to hang down. The bucket boots with turned-down tops, wide hat with plume, and tabard all add the proper flair for the adventurous masculine look.

Fashionable French Lady, ca. 1629

This drawing shows the lady's shoulders and upper bosom exposed by her broad lace-edged lingerie collar, wired to hold its shape. Her corset is high-waisted, but has a plunging stomacher. Her outer robe, called *la modeste,* is open down the front, tying just below the bosom. The skirt was called *la friponne* (hussy), and the petticoat underneath was called *la secret.* This lady's hairstyle was inspired by one worn by Anne of Austria, with fringe across the forehead, ringlets hanging down the sides, and the remainder uncut and drawn into a knot at the back of the head.

English Country Gentry, ca. 1630

Left: Shown in the Van Dyke–inspired version of the cavalier fashion, this gentleman wears a velvet jacket with slashed sleeves and passementerie (elaborate trim) Brandenburg closures down the front. The breeches are of a contrasting color and have a frontal closure of tied points. The decorative cannons below the knee are loops of ribbon, and his boot hose are embroidered lace. His embroidered Van Dyke collar is tied with band strings, and he carries a cloak. **Right:** The lady wears a taffeta gown with a lace falling band and sleeve ruffles. A matching lace-edged fichu is held in place by points at the waist. The stomacher and corset tabs match the gown in color and fabric. A beaver hat with plumes and a love-lock finish the outfit.

English Theatrical Costumes, ca. 1631

These elaborate costumes were designed by Inigo Jones for the court pantomime *Chlorinda* by dramatist Ben Jonson. The influential Jones had been the court designer/ decorator for James I and Queen Anne, and continued in that capacity for Charles I. He is best known for his architectural works, including the Banqueting House in London's Whitehall district.

French Middle-class Couple, ca. 1633

In 1633, France's Cardinal de Richelieu sought to control imports and promote French manufactured fashion goods. He brought about an edict prohibiting the wearing of gold or silver galloons, passementeries, or jeweled metallic embroidery. Thus, simplified looks, such as plain but heavy velvets and satins, became the vogue. Ribbon and thread laces became important decorative items. **Left:** The lady wears a velvet gown with a plain lingerie collar, yoke, and cuffs. She has a ribbon rosette at the bosom and waist, and a hanging cord with a small purse. The cloth headpiece is called a kerchief hood. **Right:** The gentleman wears a slashed jerkin with paned wings and sleeves, with matching breeches tied with points in front and at the waist. The decoration on his jerkin and breeches is crafted of embroidered ribbon and small buttons. He completes the look with a leather-tooled baldric, leather bucket boots, leather gauntlets, and slashed spur leathers.

French Courtiers, ca. 1633

Left: This courtier wears a velvet slashed jerkin with ribbon rosettes at the waist. The jerkin is left open to show the undershirt, and the breeches closure is tied with points. He has a plain falling band held with strings, and his sleeves end in double cuffs, plain over scalloped eyelet. **Right:** His lady wears a gown of taffeta over satin sleeves, underskirt, and stomacher. Shirred ribbon trim adorns the bodice, sleeves, and underskirt. She wears a plain, wide lingerie collar and deep lingerie cuffs, and tops the outfit with a knitted cap, rather like a tam pulled to the back.

Queen Henrietta Maria and King Charles I of England, ca. 1633

Left: England's Queen Henrietta was the sister of France's King Louis XIII, and followed the lead of the French court fashions. Here she wears a taffeta gown with an embroidered eyelet lingerie falling band, and a fichu that also tapers into embroidered eyelet fabric. The cuffs of her sleeves are gathered petals of lingerie fabric.

Right: Charles wears the cavalier look as interpreted by Van Dyck. His velvet jacket contrasts with his satin breeches, and he wears knee-high boots with the tops folded into a cuff. His broad satin baldric supports his sword and he carries long leather gauntlets.

Queen Henrietta Maria of England, ca. 1634

Here, the queen wears a satin gown with a lace and embroidery falling band. Her bodice is tied with points in the manner of the later échelle bows of the Louis XIV period. Her cuffs and gown edging are gathered sheer, as is her fan. The hair ribbon was a new touch, and again reflects the importance of ribbon in both men's and women's fashions following Richelieu's edict.

Cavalier and Lady at Piano, ca. 1635

Left: The lady wears a stiffened flat whisk over a fitted bodice which has a tabbed peplum reinforced with rows of stitching and edged with a flounce. She wears a full-length lace-edged apron in the front. Her hair is brushed up over a wire frame and held in back by a comb and bow of ribbon. **Right:** The cavalier's costume is standard for the time, with the exception of a wig with a braided and beribboned love-lock.

English Lady, ca. 1635

This illustration shows a large lawn collar with double scalloped lace edging, and a low, square décolletage. The high-waisted bodice has a long stomacher and embroidered tabs. The wings of the gown have evolved into shawl-like shoulder cover with scalloped lace edging which matches that of the deep cuffs on the full three-quarter-length sleeves.

French soldier and English soldier, ca. 1636

Left: The French soldier is wearing a ribbed doublet with sleeves that emerge from his leather overtunic. He wears slashed knee-length breeches with bunched canions of the same fabric. Accessories include a wide waist sash, leather baldric, and a neckpiece with a cross worn under his falling band. Completing the outfit are bucket boots with butterfly spur leathers. **Right:** The English soldier is wearing a wide-brimmed beaver hat trimmed with plumes, a embroidered falling collar, a metal breastplate worn over a long-skirted tunic, a fabric baldric, leather sword belt, leather gauntlets, and boots.

French Cavalier and Lady, ca. 1640

This was the period of *The Three Musketeers*, when men were quick to defend their honor and that of their lady. **Left:** This cavalier wears a doublet with paned wings and deep tabs, a shirt with paned sleeves gathered into deep cuffs, and breeches with ribbon points for frontal closure and attachment to the doublet. He wears the typical bucket boots and broad-brimmed hat. The cape with a broad collar and no sleeves is called a balagnie cloak. His sword is carried in a tooled-leather baldric. **Right:** The lady wears a cloth gown, tucked up at the sides to reveal a contrasting colored underskirt with gimp trim. Her falling band has double-scalloped lace edging, and her slashed sleeves reveal lawn undersleeves. She wears a sun mask for protection from the weather and carries a fur muff.

Common Folk, ca. 1640

This egg seller and water vendor are wearing patched clothes that have been previously owned by others. Generally, the poorer the commoner, the older and less fashionable the clothes. Nevertheless, some of the style elements worn by the upper classes are visible here, such as the man's plumed hat, the woman's underskirt, and the full sleeves of their outfits.

Common Folk, ca. 1640

This drawing shows a street wine vendor and a middle-class merchant.

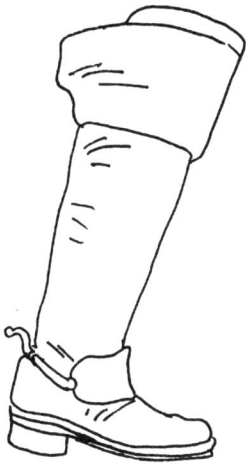
RIDING BOOT

TURNED DOWN TOP

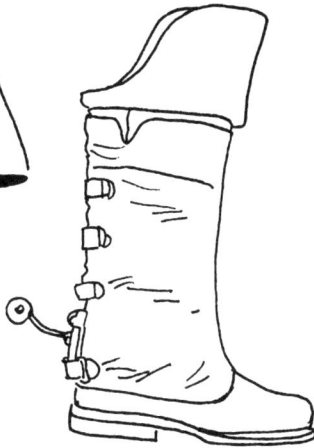
COACHMAN'S BOOT

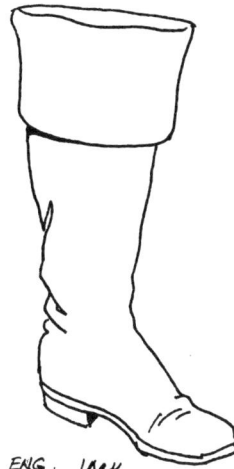
ENG. JACK
BOOT
CA 1625

CA 1625

CA 1625

1627

1629

1629

CAVALIER BOOT, RED
HEEL, PATTEN. CA 1635

LEATHER WITH EMBROIDERED
SATIN GAUNTLET
CA 1620

OPEN BUCKET
TOP BOOT
CA 1640

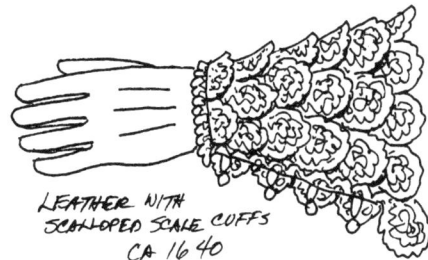
LEATHER WITH
SCALLOPED SCALE CUFFS
CA 1640

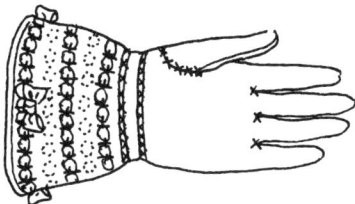
KID WITH EMBROIDERED CUFF
CA 1630

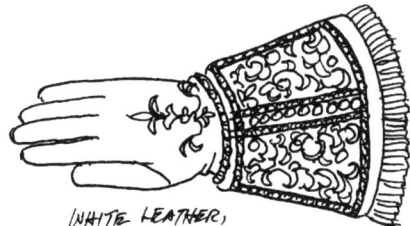
WHITE LEATHER,
GREEN & SILVER CUFFS,
FRINGE - CA 1600

Boots and Gloves

CA 1610

RIBBON ROSETTE WITH JEWEL 1612

LACE ROSETTE CA 1615

SLIPPER/PATTEN CA 1615

EMBROIDERED SILK SHOE CA 1620

CA 1620

STRIPED SILK SLIPPER RED VELVET HEEL & PANTOFLE. CA 1625

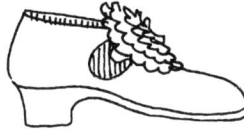

LEATHER SHOE WITH CORK SOLE & HEEL CA 1625

GATHERED RIBBON SHOE ROSE CA 1630

CA 1630

CA 1630

WHITE LEATHER-RED HEEL, JEWELED TOE CA 1633

BLACK VELVET SHOE, GREEN & SILVER BOW CA 1640

BOOT WITH TURNED DOWN TOP. CA 1635

BOOT WITH TURNED DOWN TOP & STOCKING, WORN WITH PATTEN CA 1635

WHITE LEATHER BOOT, RED HEEL. CA 1630

TURNED DOWN PLATFORM SOLED BOOT

LEATHER BOOT WHICH BUTTONED TO TRUNKS

STOCKING, RIBBON GARTER, SOCK & SHOE.

LACE EDGED BOOT HOSE - PATTEN

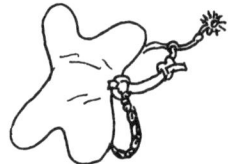

SPUR & "SPUR LEATHER" COVERING

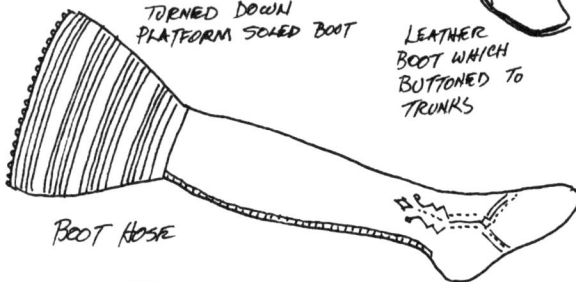

BOOT HOSE

POINT LACE FALLING BAND ENGLISH, CA 1630

FALLING RUFF 1624

GULILLA - 1620

FALLING BAND - THREAD LACE 1610

Shoes, Boots, and Collars

MILITARY
HAT
CA. 1600

JEWELED
COIF - HAIR CRIMPED &
CURLED AROUND FACE.
CA. 1600

STIFFENED BRAID
HAT. CA. 1610

"COLLET
MONTE"
(STANDING
COLLAR)
CA. 1605

PETALLED
RUFF CA. 1610

BEAVER
HAT. CA. 1610

CA. 1610

EARLY
ATTACHED
TORN-
DOWN
COLLAR
C. 1610

CA. 1610

CA. 1610

CA. 1610

CA. 1612

CA. 1610

CA. 1615

FEATHER
FAN

FOLDING
FAN

PAINTED
VELLUM
FAN

Hats, Coiffures, and Fans

STRAW HAT
CA 16

BEAVER
HAT, JEWELED
BAND CA. 1620

JEWELED
COIF,
COLLET
MONTE',
CA 1620

CA 1620

LACE CAP
CA 1620

LACE
WHISK,
PEARLS
CA. 1620

STRAW HAT
CA. 1625

CA 1620

CA 1620

CA 1628

CA 1628

Hats and Hair Ornaments

SHORT COIF WITH "LOVE-LOCK" CA. 1630

EARLY CRAVAT CA 1630

WIG WITH LOVE-LOCK CA 1630

FELT HAT, FALLING BAND (COLLAR), LOVE-LOCK

BEEF EATER STYLE CAP 1630

STREET HEAD COVER 1630

BEAVER HUNTING HAT 1630

COIF & FALLING BAND. 1630

COIF 1630

COIF WITH BOWS 1635

BOY'S CAP CA 1635

GIRL'S CAP CA 1635

CAP 1635

KERCHIEF HEAD COVER 1635

CAP 1635

COIF 1640

LADY PURITAN CA. 1640

FUR HAT CA. 1640

PURITAN HAT CA. 1640

Hats and Coiffures

Glossary

Here are definitions of terms that may be unfamiliar to modern readers:

Baldric: decorative belt worn from right shoulder to left hip, often used to hold sword or dagger

Boot hose: long linen stockings with flared tops, worn to protect silk stockings from boots

Bum roll (or barrel): a sausage-shaped pad worn at the waist to supplement the farthingale

Canions: leg coverings worn under trunk hose

Cannons: lace or ribbon frills that spill over the tops of boots

Conque: veil or shell-shaped hat made of light gauze, often worn by widows

Doublet: close-fitting, jacket-style garment worn by men

Epaulet (or epaulette): ornamental shoulder trim

Falling band: the successor to the ruff; a broad, flat-lying collar usually trimmed with lace

Farthingale: petticoat stretched over a frame to form a cone-shaped foundation under a dress. Wheel farthingales are cylindrical, with radiating spokes at the top to support the garment.

Galloon: decorative braid, sometimes made with metallic fibers

Gimp: flat, braided band used as decorative trim

Gorget: metal plate worn to protect the neck or shoulder during swordplay

Jerkin: close-fitting jacket worn by men, generally of longer length than a doublet

Love-lock: a long, curled lock of hair draped over the front of the shoulder

Panes: decorative slashes cut into garments to reveal swatches of a different-colored undergarment

Patten: wood or metal platform attached to a shoe in order to elevate the wearer's height

Peplum: bottom portion of a bodice below the waist, often sewn on as an extension, and can be pleated, tabbed, flared, decorated, or left plain

Points: ribbon ties with metal tips to make lacing easier

Ruff: stiff, pleated collar (or cuff) of varying widths and lengths. Falling ruffs lay flat over the garment.

Shoe roses: rosette shoe trim made of ribbon or lace

Slops: knee-length trunk hose, often full and unpadded

Stomacher: panel of fabric, usually patterned or decorated, worn over chest and ending in a V below the waist in front

Tabard: loose tunic with short, wide sleeves

Trunk hose: breeches worn from waist to thigh

Venetian slops: trunk hose cut extremely full and loose

Whisk: broad, flat collar often trimmed with lace. Standing whisk collars were stiffened to stand up from the shoulders.

Wings: decorative shoulder extensions attached to doublets or dresses